# GREAT SAINTS
# IN
# WORLD HISTORY

WRITTEN BY KEVIN CLARK
ILLUSTRATED BY PATRICK DIEMER

SETON PRESS
FRONT ROYAL, VA

**Executive Editor:** Dr. Mary Kay Clark
**Editors:** Seton Staff

© 2017 Seton Home Study School
All rights reserved.
Printed in the United States of America

Seton Home Study School
1350 Progress Drive
Front Royal, VA 22630
Phone: (540) 636-9990
Fax: (540) 636-1602

*For more information, visit us on the web at* www.setonhome.org.
*Contact us by e-mail at* info@setonhome.org.

ISBN: 978-1-60704-056-9

Cover: *Immaculate Conception with the Saints* by Piero di Cosimo

DEDICATED TO THE SACRED HEART OF JESUS

# Contents

# Introduction

*Great Saints in World History* contains the stories of many of the holy men and women who have had a great impact on their countries. The stories have been written to highlight some of the important accomplishments of these men and women. The drawings are the result of careful research to illustrate various historical details of the times. It is important to discuss these drawings with your child. We hope that your child will enjoy coloring each scene after the discussion of its historical significance.

*St. Peter's Basilica*

# The Worldwide Church

Do you know what the word "catholic" means? It means universal, without limit or end. There are some churches, such as the Church of England, which are for people only in a certain country. There are other churches and religions, such as the Greek Orthodox, which are only for a certain area of the world. Still other religions, such as many ancient religions, are only for the people of a certain time, and do not continue forever.

The Catholic Church is not at all like these churches. The Catholic Church is universal, which means it is meant for all countries, for all areas of the world, for all people, for all time. Wherever you can go all over the world, you will find the Catholic Church. This is because God has chosen to give His love to all people through His Church. Just as people can go to any place where God will love them, so they can go to any place where the Church will help them to save their souls.

In this book, we shall learn how the Church loves and helps people of all countries around the world. We shall see how the Church brings Christ to men all around the globe by means of holy men and women. We will see that the missionaries of the Church will travel anywhere to teach about Jesus. From the sands of Egypt, to the plains of Canada, to the bays of Ireland, to the steppes (grasslands) of Russia, all countries have their own patron saints, special saints to whom the people may pray in times of need and distress. These are the men and women whom we shall meet and walk with this year.

*St. Patrick's Cathedral, New York City*

# St. Anne: Patroness of Canada

You may think that all the saints in the Church lived after the birth of Jesus. Well, most of them did, but not all. St. Anne was the mother of the Blessed Virgin Mary, and possibly never saw Jesus, her Grandson. She is not mentioned in the New Testament, but Christian Tradition speaks of her. Tradition means the stories and teachings that Christians have told each other down through the centuries. The Catholic Church calls Anne a saint due to her great holiness in raising her holy daughter Mary.

St. Anne was married to St. Joachim, the father of Mary. Anne did not have any children until she was very old. Then Mary was born. Anne had prayed to God that He might give her a child. She promised that if she had a child, to give this child to God. A story says that God sent an angel to Anne saying, "Anne, the Lord has answered your prayer and you shalt conceive and bring forth a child, and your child shall be spoken of in all the world." Her child, Mary, the future Mother of Jesus, was born without Original Sin. This is called Mary's Immaculate Conception.

When Mary was old enough, Anne sent her to live in the Jewish temple with the holy women, just as young girls go into the convent today. This was hard for Anne because she loved Mary very much. She knew, however, that this was God's Will, and that Mary would be close to God, living and praying in the temple.

There is a great shrine dedicated to St. Anne in Quebec, Canada. It is called the shrine of St. Anne de Beaupré. It is one of the most magnificent shrines anywhere in honor of St. Anne. People from all over the world travel to the shrine to pray for favors. The shrine has published a magazine for over one hundred years, and also offers medals of St. Anne. If you are ever in Quebec, perhaps you would like to visit it.

From St. Anne, we learn patience and perseverance in prayer and the importance of sacrifice.

*Shrine of St. Anne de Beaupré*

*St. Anne presents Mary to the holy women of the temple.*

## Questions

1. St. Anne is the mother of whom? _____

   _____

2. St. Anne is spoken of through stories and teachings told through the centuries. What are these stories called?

   _____

3. Who was St. Anne's husband? _____

4. How did God let St. Anne know she would have a child?

   _____

5. What is the name of the shrine dedicated to St. Anne in

   Quebec, Canada?_____

   _____

*Ceiling of the Shrine of St. Anne de Beaupré*

# St. Thomas the Apostle: Patron of India

Thomas, the Apostle of India, is the "doubting Thomas" we read about in the Bible. After Pentecost, the Apostles went their separate ways to take the Good News of Jesus to all areas of the world. Though we cannot be totally sure, we have good evidence that St. Thomas went to preach in India.

In fact, there is a legend that St. Thomas was invited to India by a king who wanted him to build him a huge palace. The king gave Thomas a fortune with which to purchase materials and pay workmen to build a palace. Thomas took the money, but he did not build the palace. He gave all the money to the poor people of the kingdom.

The king was very angry when he found out that Thomas had given away all his money. He put Thomas in prison and was going

*The Lal Qila (Red Fort) royal palace was built between 1638 and 1648 in Delhi.*

to kill him. That night, the king received a heavenly vision saying that Thomas had built a palace in Heaven for the king, because Thomas had used the king's money to help the poor. After this, the king became a Catholic.

Recently in India, archaeologists (ar-kee-ol-o-jists), people who dig up and study ancient ruins, have found coins bearing the name of this king. On these coins is a picture of a chalice, which represents the king's conversion to Christianity.

Even though St. Thomas converted the king, he did not convert many other rich or important people in India. St. Thomas preached mainly to the poor, so the rich people thought his religion was for the poor. The nobles in India were called "Brahmins" (brom-mins). They thought that any ground Thomas walked on was cursed (but, in reality, it was blessed). Suddenly, some of the Brahmin priests attacked and killed St. Thomas with a spear.

From St. Thomas, we learn the virtue of perseverance. Thomas was never able to make India a Catholic country, but he never stopped trying. Today, Mother Teresa's Sisters of Charity are continuing to help people in India, just as St. Thomas did.

*Taj Mahal, Agra, India*

*St. Thomas gives the king's money to the poor.*

## Questions

1. Where did St. Thomas go to preach after Pentecost?

   _____

2. What did St. Thomas do with the money given to him by a king in India? _____

3. Why did the king not kill Thomas after putting him in prison?

   _____

   _____

4. Why did rich people think the religion of St. Thomas was for the poor? _____

5. What did the Brahmin priests think about the ground on which St. Thomas walked? _____

*Presidential Palace in New Delhi*

# St. Denis: Patron of France

St. Denis is a saint whose life is a mystery. Not everyone can agree on everything that he did, or even what his whole name was. He is called St. Denis, sometimes St. Dionysius (di-oh-nee-see-us). All the ancient legends do agree that he traveled to France, even to Paris, though it was not called Paris at the time, to preach the Gospel.

Most experts agree that St. Denis was the Dionysius who became a Christian when St. Paul preached in Athens. In the Bible, Acts 17:34 says, "Certain persons, however, joined him (Paul) and became believers; among them were Dionysius the Areopagite and a woman named Damaris and others with them." The legend says that Denis became the first bishop of Athens and was a close friend of the Apostle John. Denis was known for his great mercy to sinners. He once told the following story to those who, in vengeance, wanted to see God's anger brought down on sinners.

*Notre Dame - side view*

11

*St. Denis preaches to the people of Athens, where he was bishop for many years.*

12

There was once a priest named Carpus who wished that certain sinners would be sent to Hell. That night, the priest dreamed that these people were being dragged into Hell. He was very happy until he saw Jesus come down from Heaven and try to pull the sinners back. Jesus said to Carpus, "Strike Me, if you will, Carpus, and take out your anger on Me. I will die a second time for men." Carpus then knew that he should not pray for justice for sinners, but for mercy.

St. Denis was bishop of Athens for many years, the legends say. Then he became a missionary and traveled to Spain and France, which was called "Gaul" at the time. He became bishop of Paris and was martyred there. A monastery was built at the point where he is said to have been martyred. The kings of France were buried in that same monastery for many hundreds of years. The monastery of St. Denis is one of the great shrines in France.

*Basilica of St. Denis*

From St. Denis, we learn the importance of compassion for our fellow men. Just as Jesus wept when He heard of the death of Lazarus, so we should weep when we see sinners dying. We should always ask God to be merciful to sinners. Then we ourselves shall receive mercy from Jesus.

## Questions

1. Is there much mystery surrounding St. Denis' life and even his name? _____

2. What is another name for St. Denis? _____

3. In the story about Carpus, what do we learn we should pray for? _____

4. Is St. Denis a martyr? _____

5. Who else was buried in the monastery built for St. Denis?

   _____

   _____

*Cathedral of Chartres, France*

# St. Nicholas: Patron of Russia

Did you know that "Santa Claus" means "Saint Nicholas"? Saint Nicholas was known for giving secret gifts during the night. He was a very rich man, and he wanted to use his money to help the poor. One day, he heard that a poor man did not have enough money to have weddings for his three daughters. St. Nicholas felt sorry for the father. That night, he went to the man's house and secretly threw a bag of gold through the window. The next night, St. Nicholas threw in another bag for the man's second daughter.

After receiving the second bag, the father of the girls decided to wait by the window to see who was throwing in the bags. When Nicholas came the next night with a bag of gold for the man's last daughter, the father chased him down the street and caught him. The father wanted to tell everyone of the good deed that Nicholas had done, but Nicholas begged the man not to tell. Nicholas did not want to receive praise on Earth for what he had done. Nicholas wanted his reward to be in Heaven.

*The Kremlin, Moscow, Russia*

*Bishop Saint Nicholas leaves a gift for the poor.*

*Cathedral of St. Basil, Moscow*

Nicholas lived in the city of Myra in Asia Minor in the fourth century after the birth of Christ. One day, the bishop of this city died. The other bishops in the area came together to decide who should take his place. One of these bishops had a heavenly vision that the first man to come through the church door the next day should be the new bishop. The heavenly vision said that this man would be named Nicholas. The next day, Nicholas was the first man in the church. The bishop said to him, "What is your name?" He said to the bishop, "Nicholas, the servant of Your Holiness." Then they made Nicholas the new bishop.

St. Nicholas was well-known even during his lifetime because so many people received miracles through him. After he died, he appeared to many people who asked for his help in difficulties. One time, when the Roman emperor Constantine had condemned some innocent men to death, the men prayed for Nicholas to help them. Then Nicholas appeared in a vision to Constantine and told him that the men were innocent. Constantine freed them.

From St. Nicholas, we learn that gifts should be given in love. We should not think about what we may receive in return. It is God who will reward us for our good deeds.

*St. Isaac's Cathedral, St. Petersburg, Russia*

## Questions

1. What does "Santa Claus" mean?_____

2. Nicholas did not want the father of the three girls to tell anyone about his good deed. Where did he want his reward?

   _____

   _____

3. Nicholas became the bishop in the city of Myra because one of the bishops had a vision. What was the Myra bishop told in his vision?

   _____

4. What was St. Nicholas well known for during his lifetime?

   _____

5. Why did Constantine free the innocent men he had

   condemned to death? _____

   _____

*St. Petersburg*

19

# St. Patrick: Patron of Ireland

St. Patrick was born in the Roman province of Britannia, what is now Wales and England, around the year 387. Julius Caesar had begun the first expedition to Britannia in the century before Jesus was born. By 387, over 400 years later, Britannia was a thriving Roman civilization. Patrick's father was a Roman citizen. When Patrick was still a teenager, only sixteen or seventeen years old, Patrick was captured by pirates and carried off to pagan Ireland. How frightening it must have been for Patrick to be separated from his family and taken to a strange land!

Patrick had not been a very good Catholic in his native land, but in Ireland, he had much time to think. He began praying to Jesus one hundred times during the day and one hundred times during the night. St. Patrick wrote that in this way, "My faith grew and my spirit was stirred up." After a few years, he was able to escape from his master in Ireland, and he returned to Britannia.

*Galway Cathedral*

Patrick could not forget God's children in Ireland. There were a few Catholics in Ireland, but most of the people were still pagan. Patrick knew that God was calling him to be a missionary to the Irish. The Pope had already sent a bishop to Ireland, but the bishop had left without making many converts. After Patrick prepared and studied for many years, the Pope appointed him the new bishop of Ireland.

Patrick already knew the language and the customs of the Irish people, so he was quickly accepted by them. He was able to convert the chiefs of the tribes, and with their help, the people became Catholic.

St. Patrick set up monasteries and convents so that men and women could lead holy lives. These grew rapidly, and soon Ireland had the greatest monasteries in all of Europe. From these monasteries, holy monks traveled all over Europe, even to America, in search of people to teach about Jesus. Today, Ireland is one of the greatest Catholic countries in the world.

From St. Patrick, we learn the virtue of forgiveness. He did not hate his Irish captors, but loved them enough to dedicate his life to them. We also should follow the words of Christ and "love those who persecute" us, or who perhaps tease us or laugh at us.

*Dublin Castle*

*Irish tribal chiefs listen to St. Patrick talk about the one true Church.*

22

*Exterior*

*St. Patrick's Cathedral in Dublin was built on the spot where St. Patrick baptized the first pagans.*

*Interior*

## Questions

1. When Patrick was only sixteen or seventeen years old, who captured him? _____

2. Where did they take him?_____

3. How many times during the day and night did Patrick pray?

   _____

4. What was God calling Patrick to be? _____

5. What did St. Patrick set up in Ireland?_____

   _____

# St. Augustine of Canterbury: Patron of England

In the years after St. Patrick, a terrible tragedy befell the Roman empire. Tribes coming from Germany and eastern Europe swept down over the Roman provinces and took over parts of the empire. These tribes cut off Britain from the rest of the empire and eventually took Britain over for themselves. For many years, the people in Britain had very little contact with the rest of the world. Then, in the year 596, Pope Gregory asked St. Augustine to lead a mission to the people in Britain.

Augustine was received by Ethelbert, the king of a province in England called Kent. Soon Ethelbert joined the Catholic Church. Pope Gregory instructed Augustine that he was not to tear down the buildings that had been used as pagan temples.

*Canterbury Cathedral*

Instead, he told St. Augustine to turn those buildings into Catholic churches. In Canterbury, St. Augustine built a cathedral, and he became the archbishop of Canterbury. Until the Protestants seized the churches during the Protestant Revolution, Canterbury was the main cathedral of England. This means that the bishop there was the most honored and respected bishop in the country.

There were in Britain at this time some people who had remained Catholic but who had not been in contact with the Pope for many years. At first, these Christians did not like the idea of being under Bishop Augustine. Finally, in 664, at the Synod (meeting of Church leaders) of Whitby, these Catholics accepted the authority of Bishop Augustine, the representative of the Pope.

Because of the work of St. Augustine, the Catholic Faith spread all over England, among both the rich and the poor. England remained for many years a strongly Catholic country, until King Henry VIII rebelled against the Church in the 1500s.

From St. Augustine, we learn how important it is to share our faith with others, even if they think they do not want to hear it.

*Mosaic of St. Augustine from Westminster Cathedral, London*

*St. Augustine arrives in Britain.*

## Questions

1. Who asked St. Augustine to lead a mission to the people of Britain?

   _____

2. What did St. Augustine do to the buildings that had been used

   as pagan temples? _____

   _____

3. Where was St. Augustine the archbishop?_____

4. Whom had the people of Britain not been in contact with for

   many years? _____

5. Did the Catholic Faith spread all over England because of

   St. Augustine? _____

*Big Ben and Parliament, London*

*Bishop Willibrord shows the people the error of superstition.*

# St. Willibrord: Patron of Holland

St. Willibrord was born in England in the year 658, sixty years after St. Augustine of Canterbury had begun his work of conversion. St. Willibrord lived in Northumbria, which is a province in the northeastern part of England. St. Willibrord knew how important a good education was, so he studied in a monastery in the town of Ripon for twelve years.

At this time, England was such a strong Catholic land that it could send out its own missionaries to other areas. In the year 690, Willibrord received permission from the Pope to preach in northern Germany. This area was called "Friesland" (freez-land). When the Pope made Willibrord a bishop, Willibrord made his "see" (the place where a bishop lives) in the city of Utrecht, now located in the Netherlands.

*Utrecht Cathedral, the Netherlands (side and back)*

Willibrord tried to preach in Denmark, but the king of the province would not allow it. On his way back by ship, St. Willibrord was blown onto an island named Heligoland. This island was considered sacred by the Danes (the people of Denmark) and by the pagans in Friesland. It was supposedly forbidden by the Danish "gods" to kill any animal or eat any plant found on the island. St. Willibrord killed some of the plants and small animals for food to show the people the error of their beliefs, but unfortunately many people still held to their pagan superstitions.

Today in Holland, Willibrord is honored by a procession which is held each year on the Tuesday before Pentecost. This procession has been held in the city of Echternach every year since 1553. In the procession, the people, walking four or more together, hold hands and dance through the streets. When they reach the shrine of St. Willibrord, they receive a blessing. This procession is to ask God for favors for the sick and to make reparation for sin.

From St. Willibrord, we learn that it is important to learn about God. We must first study our Faith in our catechism before we can share it with others.

*Amsterdam, the Netherlands*

## Questions

1. Where was St. Willibrord born? _____

2. Was this a strong Catholic land at this time? _____

3. What did St. Willibrord do to show the people of Heligoland the error of their beliefs?_____

   _____

4. Did all of the people believe him?

   _____

5. What do the people do during the procession honoring St. Willibrord? _____

   _____

   _____

*Ripon Monastery, England*

*St. Boniface proves to the pagans that their "gods" do not exist.*

# St. Boniface: Patron of Germany

Imagine that you are a member of a pagan German tribe in the year 723. A Catholic missionary named Boniface has come to tell you about Jesus Christ, whom he teaches in the Son of God. The elders of your tribe do not believe him. They believe that there is a pagan "god" who lives in a special oak tree on the mountain. Now Boniface has said that he will cut down the tree. Everyone around you says that if Boniface touches the tree, he will be struck down by the gods. Boniface starts chopping at the tree, and the people stand in awe. Suddenly, the tree topples. Boniface remains standing. Everyone then begins to ask Boniface about the true God, Jesus Christ.

*Fulda Cathedral is where St. Boniface is buried.*

St. Boniface was born in England in 680. He was from a noble family and studied at a great monastery in England. At the monastery, he took time to learn the Scriptures well. He was a brilliant man, and soon he began to rise to important positions in the English Church. Boniface might have gained great fame in England, but he had a great desire to take the Gospel to pagans.

Boniface journeyed to Rome in 718 and convinced Pope Gregory to send him to Germany. Irish missionaries had gone to Germany many years before, but the churches they left had not continued. Boniface, however, had great perseverance. Though the Irish missionaries had come and left, Boniface would not leave the German people. He found so much work to do that he sent requests to England for more missionaries. From England came many holy monks and nuns to help him. Because of his hard work and great success, Boniface was made archbishop of all Germany.

From St. Boniface, we learn about the courage one must have to go to a strange land and teach the people about God. We should remember the zeal and courage of Boniface when we have an opportunity to share our Catholic Faith.

*German Parliament, Berlin*

## Questions

1. Where did the elders of the tribe think the pagan "god" lived?

   _____

2. What did St. Boniface do to the oak tree?

   _____

3. In what country was St. Boniface born?

   _____

4. Where did St. Boniface want to go so badly that he asked Pope Gregory to allow him? _____

5. Who came to help St. Boniface with his work?

   _____

*Marienplatz, Munich, Germany, is named after the Blessed Mother on the monument.*

# St. Wenceslaus: Patron of Czechoslovakia

You have probably heard the song "Good King Wenceslaus." Did you ever wonder who King Wenceslaus was? Wenceslaus was born in 907 in Prague, which is now the capital city of the Czech (pronounced "check") Republic. His parents were Ratislav and Drahomira, the rulers of Bohemia. Bohemia is southwest of Poland and southeast of Germany. It is part of the Czech Republic now, but it used to be part of Czechoslovakia (check-o-slow-vock-ee-a). Before that, it was an independent kingdom.

The grandmother of Wenceslaus was St. Ludmilla. Along with her husband, she had brought Catholicism into Bohemia. The mother of Wenceslaus, however, did not accept Catholicism and tried to return the country to paganism. She tried to prevent Wenceslaus from taking his proper place as king. With help from the Catholics in Bohemia, however, Wenceslaus did become king. He did not hold any grudge against his mother, but treated her well for the rest of her life. He was a good and kind king who loved to attend Mass.

*St. Vitus Cathedral, Prague*

Wenceslaus was murdered by his own brother, Boleslaus, who wanted to be king. In September of 929, Boleslaus invited Wenceslaus to a party. Wenceslaus was told by his advisors that he would be in danger, but Wenceslaus would not believe them. On his way to Mass, the day after the party, Boleslaus and his friends attacked Wenceslaus and killed him. The last words of Wenceslaus were, "Brother, may God forgive you."

Wenceslaus had been much loved by the people, and they immediately regarded him as a martyr for Christ. His body was taken to the Church of St. Vitus in Prague. Many miracles were worked there through the intercession of St. Wenceslaus. The people soon regarded him as the patron saint of Bohemia, and many years later, he was named the patron of Czechoslovakia.

From St. Wenceslaus, we learn that we must do what is right, even at the risk of our lives. God will care for us, and if we should give our lives for Him, our reward will be great in Heaven.

*Wenceslaus Chapel in St. Vitus Cathedral*

*St. Wenceslaus is attacked.*

## Questions

1. Who were Ratislav and Drahomira, the rulers of Bohemia?

   _____

2. What made Wenceslaus' grandmother special?

   _____

3. Who tried to prevent Wenceslaus from taking his place as king?

   _____

4. Who murdered Wenceslaus? _____

5. Where was Wenceslaus going when Boleslaus and his friends

   attacked him? _____

*Prague*

# Saints Cyril and Methodius: Co-patrons of Europe

Saints Cyril and Methodius were brothers who were born in Thessalonica in the ninth century (the 800s). Thessalonica is the city in Greece to which St. Paul sent two epistles, or letters, which we can read in the Bible. Early in life, the brothers gained a reputation for being very learned and holy men. One day, the prince of Moravia asked that missionaries be sent to his people to teach them the Faith in their own language, called Slavonic. Moravia is a province of the Czech Republic, directly south of Poland and southeast of Germany. The people who live there are called Slavs. Cyril and Methodius were chosen to be the missionaries to the Slavs in Moravia.

Cyril and Methodius discovered that the Slavonic language had no alphabet. This meant that the language could be spoken but not written. Cyril devised an alphabet for the Slavs. This

*St. Barbara Church, Kutna Hora, Moravia*

is called the Cyrillic alphabet and is the basis for the Russian alphabet of today. The Slavs were happy to be taught in their own language, and the brothers made many converts. Unfortunately, they had problems with some German bishops in the area, who did not want the people to hear Mass in Slavonic. They thought that the Mass should be said only in Latin or Greek.

Cyril and Methodius journeyed to Rome to ask for the support of the Pope. They brought along with them the relics of Pope St. Clement, an early martyr of the Church who had died in exile. Pope Adrian II decided to support the brothers. He made them bishops and said that they could say the Mass in Slavonic. However, Cyril never made it back to Moravia but died in Rome. His body was buried in the Church of St. Clement in Rome.

Methodius returned to Moravia to be bishop there. Once again, however, the German bishops tried to stop him. They actually put Bishop Methodius in jail! The Pope finally obtained his release from the disobedient German bishops.

During his last years, Methodius completed a translation of the Bible into Slavonic. He died on Tuesday of Holy Week in 885.

After years of devotion to the holy brothers by the Slavonic people, Saints Cyril and Methodius were named patrons of Moravia. In 1980, Pope John Paul II named them co-patrons of Europe, along with St. Benedict.

From Saints Cyril and Methodius, we learn that our work might not always be easy. We may be hindered even by people of our own Faith. It is more important, however, that we try to do God's work than that we receive approval from our friends.

*St. Matthias Church, Budapest*

*St. Cyril works on the alphabet for the Slavonic language
while his brother, St. Methodius, studies the newly written words.*

## Questions

1. Were Saints Cyril and Methodius related?

   _____

2. Did they have a good reputation early in life? _____

   _____

3. What did Cyril and Methodius discover about the Slavonic

   language? _____

4. Did Pope Adrian II decide to support the brothers concerning

   saying the Mass in Slavonic? _____

5. What did Methodius translate into Slavonic during his last

   years? _____

*St. Barbara Church, Kutna Hora, Moravia (side view)*

# St. Stephen: Patron of Hungary

St. Stephen was born around 975 to a tribe of people called the Magyars. These were nomads, people who moved from place to place. They had lived in Russia, but they migrated into Hungary. Stephen's father and mother were the Magyar king and queen. At birth, Stephen was named Vaik, but when he was baptized in 986, he took the name Stephen. Later, he became King Stephen.

Most of the leading men in Hungary were baptized around this time. Many of them did not really believe in the Catholic religion, but Stephen was a firm believer. Some of the nobles did not even pretend to be Catholic. They wanted to keep their pagan ways and their pagan sins. These pagan men raised an army and marched against King Stephen. Even though he was outnumbered, Stephen won a great victory against them at the Battle of Veszprem in 998.

*St. Stephen's Church, Budapest*

Although Stephen was a Catholic, he had little contact with the Pope since Hungary was so far from Rome. Stephen decided to write and ask the Pope to officially declare him king. The Pope did this and sent a beautiful crown to Stephen as a sign of his authority. This crown has been a symbol of Hungary ever since then. It is called the Crown of St. Stephen or the Holy Crown of Hungary. Stephen certainly merited the trust of the Pope. He was a good example of a Catholic king. He was always concerned about his people, and made a vow never to refuse giving alms

*Crown of St. Stephen on display at the Hungarian National Museum in Budapest*

*The Pope sent a beautiful crown to St. Stephen as a sign of his authority.*

(money) to those in need. He was always very merciful with his enemies, even those who tried to murder him.

What has become of the crown of St. Stephen? When the Nazis invaded Hungary during World War II, they stole the crown and took it out of the country. After the war, it was given to the United States government, which kept it for many years. In 1978, the United States returned the crown to Hungary. Hungarians were very much opposed to this. The crown of St. Stephen is the symbol of Hungary, and Hungarians did not want it to be in the hands of the godless Communist government which ruled the country at that time.

From St. Stephen, we learn how important it is that we go to the Pope for guidance. The Pope is guided by the Holy Spirit in matters of faith and morals. When those around us fail, we can always look to the Pope as a sure beacon of truth.

*High altar in Esztergom Basilica, Esztergom, Hungary*

## Questions

1. Nomads are people who do what?_____
_____

2. Was Stephen a firm believer when he was baptized?
_____

3. What did the Pope send to Stephen as a sign of his authority?
_____

4. Was St. Stephen merciful with his enemies?_____
_____

5. Who stole St. Stephen's crown?_____

*Budapest, Hungary*

48

# St. Francis of Assisi: Patron of Italy

St. Francis of Assisi must surely be one of the most loved saints in all history. He is honored by non-Catholics and even non-Christians for his love and charity. A collection of the stories and legends about St. Francis would fill many books. The books written about him would fill many bookshelves.

St. Francis was born in 1181 in Assisi, a town in the central part of Italy. His father was a rich merchant, so he grew up in the midst of great wealth. In his early years, he spent all his time having fun. He did not commit serious sins at this time; he just did not care about anything except having a good time. He was a good-hearted man, though, and gave much of his money to charity.

*St. Francis of Assisi Basilica, Assisi, Italy*

Francis wanted to be a soldier. However, one day while Francis was engaged in his military duties, God sent heavenly visions to him directing him to return to his home. When Francis began to think about his life, he decided that he would work constantly on gaining holiness. He did this by praying and working with the sick and poor of the city. He gave away his fancy clothes to the poor and began to wear old clothes himself. He would give away money and food, and then beg for his own food. His father became very angry when he found this out. When Francis refused to change his activities, he said Francis was no longer to be considered his son.

Francis continued his begging because he believed that it would please Jesus for him not to be attached to worldly things.

One day, Francis heard the words of the Gospel about giving up everything for Christ. So he gave everything he had to the poor except for his robe and his sandals. Many people recognized his holiness and began to follow him. Some men asked Francis to let them join him and live as he lived. This is how the order of the Franciscans began.

Throughout his life, Francis worked many miracles through the power of Jesus. He was able to control the animals and talk to them. He is said to have tamed a vicious wolf in one city and to have asked the sparrows to be quiet while he preached. Very often, he cured the sick who were brought to him. His most precious gift from Jesus was the "stigmata." This means that he miraculously received the same wounds in his hands, feet, and side which our Lord suffered. Francis died in 1226 after many illnesses.

*San Ruffino is where St. Francis was baptized.*

*St. Francis preaches to his rich friends in his hometown.*

51

From St. Francis, we learn the importance of poverty. Even if we own many things, we can still live in spiritual poverty. This means that we love God above all things and we use what we own for His honor and glory. If God takes all our possessions away from us, we should think nothing of it. For if we have Jesus, we have everything.

*Papal Altar of the Lower Basilica in St. Francis Assisi Church*

## Questions

1. Was St. Francis' father rich or poor? _____

2. What did Francis want to be before God directed him in a vision?

   _____

3. Did Francis give away his food, money, and clothes to the

   poor?_____

4. Was Francis' father happy or angry with this? _____

5. What kind of miracles could Francis perform?

   _____

   _____

*Venice, Italy*

53

# St. Elizabeth: Patroness of Portugal

Have you ever thought about what it would be like to be a prince or a princess? Do you think that it would be fun all the time? Well, it might be fun, but it also could be very hard, as St. Elizabeth of Portugal could tell you.

Elizabeth was born in 1271 in a city in Spain named Saragossa. Her father was Don Pedro, son of King Jayme of Aragon. She had all the Earthly riches that a little girl could want, but her parents were not good Catholics. The court (the king's household) was not a good place for a young girl to learn her Faith and practice the virtues. Despite this, as she grew in size, she also grew in holiness.

*Imperial Park and the Monastery of the Jeronimos, Lisbon*

Elizabeth desired above all things that she might join a convent to dedicate her life to Jesus. Things are not always so easy for a princess, however. In those days, marriages were sometimes "arranged." This means that Elizabeth was not allowed to choose whom she would marry. Instead, her father decided this. Elizabeth could have refused to marry the man her father chose for her. She decided, though, that God would be most pleased if she obediently followed her father's wishes.

Elizabeth was married to King Diniz of Portugal. He was not a very good Catholic, but he was kind and understanding with his people. He was a good and wise ruler who made just laws and ruled his kingdom fairly. Queen Elizabeth certainly had much to do with this. She was very happy to give food and money to the needy people. In the city of Coimbra, she built a school to teach young orphan girls how to farm. At the weddings of these girls to local farmers, Queen Elizabeth would give them farm land as a wedding gift. This is only one example of Elizabeth's charity and wisdom.

*Inside the Monastery of the Jeronimos*

*St. Elizabeth, Queen of Portugal, assists her husband, King Diniz, to arrange peace with his enemy.*

56

Elizabeth was concerned with many matters in her years as queen, but she was most concerned that peace be maintained. She constantly asked her husband to talk rather than fight. Sometimes she herself would arrange peace treaties.

After the death of her husband, Elizabeth joined the convent of the Poor Clares. She did not become a sister in the order, but she lived with them according to their rule. She did not become a Poor Clare, because she felt that she must continue her rule as queen.

From Elizabeth of Portugal, we learn how those in authority should act. They should use their authority for the benefit of others, and not for their own personal gain.

*Church of Bom Jesus do Monte, near Braga, Portugal*

## Questions

1. Did St. Elizabeth possess many Earthly riches as young girl?

   _____

2. Were St. Elizabeth's parents good Catholics? _____

3. What is an arranged marriage?_____

   _____

4. What was St. Elizabeth's main concern as a queen?

   _____

5. What did St. Elizabeth do after her husband's death?

   _____

*Batalha Monastery*

# St. Bridget: Patroness of Sweden

St. Bridget was born in Sweden in 1303. Her father was the governor of the province of Upland. When she was a very young girl, she had a vision of Christ. She saw Him hanging upon a cross, and He said to her, "Look upon Me, my daughter." She said to Him, "Alas, who has treated You thus?" He replied, "They who despise Me, and spurn My love for them."

Bridget was married at the age of fourteen to Ulf Gudmarsson. They lived happily in marriage for twenty-eight years, and she gave birth to eight children. One of her daughters was canonized as St. Catherine of Sweden. This shows that even in a large family, with many activities, there can be plenty of time for God.

In 1335, Bridget went to the court of King Magnus II of Sweden to be a "lady-in-waiting" to the queen. She tried to be a good influence on the king and queen, since they were not leading very holy lives. While living there, she received many revelations from God. Some revelations were personal favors for her, but others revealed future events between countries. She counseled the king as much as she could, but often he would not listen to her.

When Bridget's husband died in 1344, she decided to become a nun. After a heavenly vision, she started the Order of the Most Holy Savior, also called the Bridgettines. At this time, the Pope had left Rome and was living in France at a city named Avignon. Bridget tried her best to convince the Pope to return to Rome. She even went to live in Rome to comfort the people there who were without their papal ruler. Bridget died in Rome on July 23, 1373. Finally, in 1377, Pope Gregory XI did return to Rome, four years after her death.

St. Bridget is most famous today for her book *Revelations*, which contains the private revelations given to her by Our Lord Jesus Christ and His Blessed Mother. This book was first published in 1492, the year Columbus discovered America. It was translated into English in 1531, and has been read and prayed for close to 500 years!

From the revelations given to St. Bridget, we learn the suffering which sin causes Christ. Let us be sure that we are never part of "They who despise Me and spurn My love."

*First page of St. Bridget's Book,* Revelations

*St. Bridget founded the religious order called the Bridgettines.*

## Questions

1.  Who appeared to Bridget when she was a young girl?

    _____

2.  What happened when St. Bridget was fourteen?

    _____

3.  What relation was St. Catherine of Sweden to St. Bridget?

    _____

4.  What did St. Bridget do after her husband died?

    _____

5.  What kind of a book did St. Bridget write?

    _____

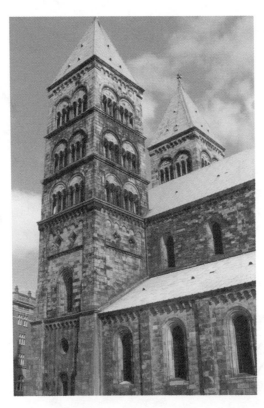

*Lund Cathedral, Sweden*

# St. Francis Xavier: Patron of the Orient

Does it surprise you that one man should be the patron saint of so many countries? St. Francis Xavier is an extraordinary saint. Many men in his day went exploring in search of gold, but Francis explored in search of souls. Francis desired above all things that every person in every land might hear the words of life and know the mercy of Jesus.

Francis Xavier was born in the year 1506 in a town along the border of France and Spain. He was a very smart boy and was sent to study at the greatest university in the world, the University of Paris. At the university, Francis met St. Ignatius Loyola and became one of the first members of the Society of Jesus, or the Jesuits, started by St. Ignatius.

*Imperial Palace*

63

*St. Francis Xavier blesses a new friend while visiting Japan.*

You know that Christopher Columbus discovered America in 1492. This encouraged others to sail out to discover new lands. By the time Francis became a Jesuit priest, the country of Portugal had made many settlements in India. The king of Portugal asked that Jesuits be sent as missionaries to India. That is how Francis Xavier arrived in India in 1542 to preach the Gospel.

Xavier found, however, that before he could preach the Gospel to the Indians, he had to preach it to the Portuguese! These men, far from home, and far from law and order, were not following the Ten Commandments, but were stealing from and cheating the Indians. Xavier tried to make them realize that they could not escape the Laws of God, no matter how far they traveled.

*Tokyo with Mount Fuji in the Background*

Francis worked in India for many years and also traveled to the many islands around India, preaching about Jesus. Then he heard about the islands to the north called Japan. He was soon able to find a boat and to sail to the islands. In Japan, he established communities, which later survived through years of persecutions in which all the priests in the country were killed.

While still in Japan, St. Francis Xavier heard of the country of China. He believed he should convert the people in China also, though it was not safe in China at that time. Any European who visited there risked death. However, before Francis Xavier reached China, Jesus called the saint to his heavenly home. He died of a fever while waiting for permission to enter China.

From St. Francis Xavier, we learn that we should always be ready to sacrifice in order to bring the Gospel to men. We should never be too tired to tell people about Jesus.

*Himeji Castle, Japan*

## Questions

1. St. Francis Xavier did not explore in search for gold, but in search for what? _____

2. St. Francis Xavier joined the Society of Jesus when he was at the University of Paris. What is another name for this society?

   _____

3. Where did St. Francis Xavier go to preach the Gospel before traveling to Japan? _____

4. Was China a safe place for Xavier to go to preach? Why?

   _____

   _____

5. Did St. Francis Xavier ever go to China as he wished? Why?

   _____

   _____

*Scenic Japan*

*St. Rose of Lima, even as a young child, showed signs of great holiness.*

# St. Rose of Lima: Patroness of Latin America and the Philippines

St. Rose of Lima is one of the first saints born in America after it was discovered by Christopher Columbus. Rose was born on April 20, 1586 in Lima (lee-ma), a city in Peru. Even as a young child, she showed signs of great holiness. Like a hermit, she took herself away from other people to be alone with God. She made a shed or hut in her backyard and spent many hours there alone in prayer. In this shed, the Baby Jesus would often appear to her.

*Cuzco Cathedral, Peru*

When Rose was still a young girl, her family moved to a mining town. The life there was cruel and hard for the miners. Rose did all that she could to help them. She worked so hard that she became very ill. Her family had to move away. It was many months before she fully recovered.

When she grew to become a lovely young lady, many men wanted to marry Rose, but instead Rose joined the third order of St. Dominic in Lima. While there, she met St. Martin de Porres, who also lived and worked in Lima. While Martin worked to help the poor of the city, Rose prayed for his success. Her life in the convent was one of simple prayer and sacrifice. After a long illness, St. Rose died on August 24, 1617. She was thirty-one years old, but she had influenced many people by her acts of kindness.

From St. Rose, we learn the importance of a quiet life of prayer and penance. Some people think that to do important things, one must go into the world and be famous. Prayer and fasting are more important. Greater things are accomplished by a person in constant prayer than by any president or king.

*Archbishop's residence, Lima*

## Questions

1. Did St. Rose show signs of holiness as a child? How?

   _____

   _____

2. What happened to St. Rose when her family moved to a mining

   town?_____

3. Did many men want to marry St. Rose when she was a young

   woman? _____

4. What did St. Rose decide to do with her life?_____

   _____

5. What important thing do we learn from St. Rose?

   _____

*Manila Cathedral, Philippines*

*St. Peter Claver comforts newly arrived slaves.*

# St. Peter Claver: Patron of Colombia

The year is 1630, and we are standing at a port in South America as a slave ship is docking. These ships carry men crowded like animals in cages. Many of the slaves die on the way from Africa to America. Those that arrive are sick and starved, and many more of them will die. We cannot stand the sight, so we turn away. Up the road, we see a priest walking toward the ship. He is bringing blankets and medicine for the slaves. As we watch, he goes to the slaves, cleans them, and cares for their wounds. We see him hold in his arms the poor men with terrible diseases. This is St. Peter Claver, caring for the slaves, as he did for 38 years.

*Bogota Cathedral, Colombia*

If we had seen Peter Claver earlier in his life, we would have doubted that such a man could ever be named a saint. He felt his vocation at an early age, but he was terribly frightened of following it. He wanted to join the Jesuits, but he did not want to take a lifelong vow. He would rather have worked as a layman for Jesus, but God wanted him to be a priest.

Although Peter was hesitant about taking on his work, he was untiring once he started. We can hardly believe that a man could show such love until we realize that it was done only through the power of God. Even sickness could not stop St. Peter. Sometimes when he was too sick to sit up straight, his friends had to tie him onto his horse so that he could go and see his people.

When St. Peter Claver died, the people knew he was a saint. Many broke into his room and took pieces of his clothing or bits of his possessions. It was as if they hoped to hold onto a piece of God by holding something that had belonged to St. Peter Claver. Indeed, God was in St. Peter Claver and in everything he did.

From St. Peter Claver, we learn that we must die to ourselves and follow the Will of God. It may be hard for us sometimes, but only in this way can we have true happiness in this world and in the next world.

*Christ the Redeemer, Rio de Janeiro, Brazil*

## Questions

1. How did St. Peter take care of the slaves that came in on the ships from Africa to America? _____

_____

2. Was St. Peter scared of becoming a priest when he was a young man?

_____

3. Was St. Peter entirely devoted to his work?_____

4. What did St. Peter's friends do when he was sick and he could not sit up straight? _____

_____

5. What did people do after St. Peter died?_____

_____

*Fortress at San Fernando, Cartagena, Colombia*

# Map of Europe

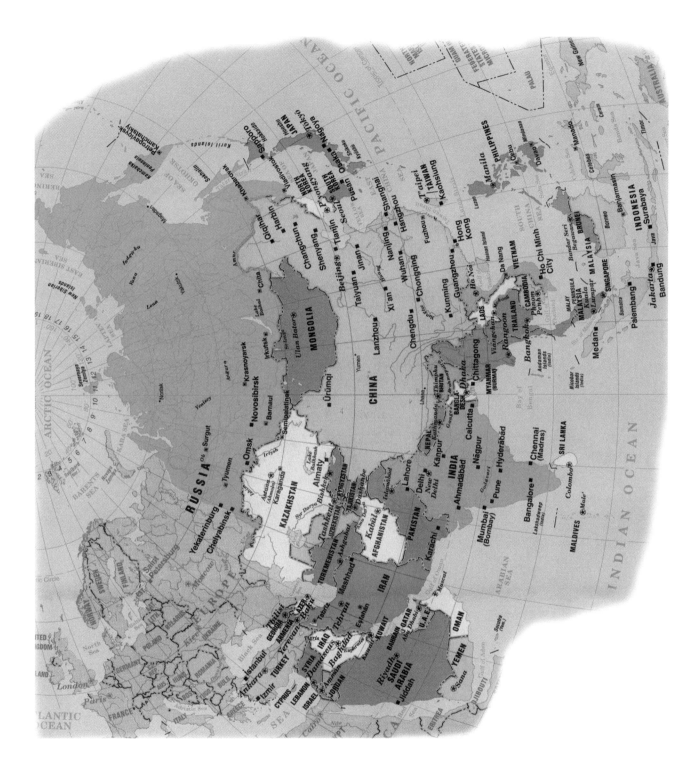

Map of Asia

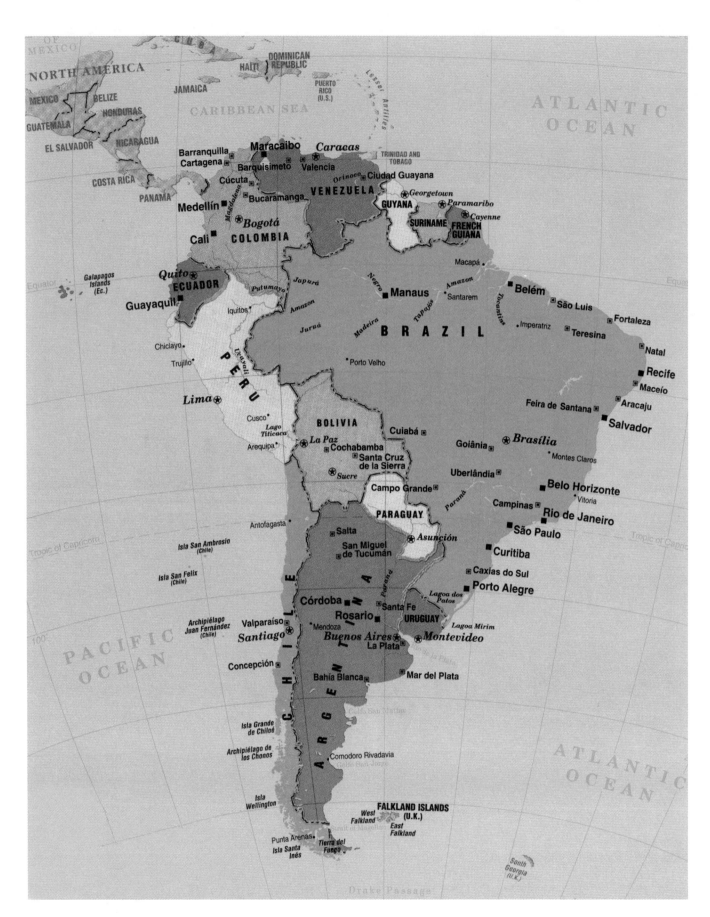

# Map of South America

# Great Saints in World History
## Workbook Answer Key

**St. Anne: Patroness of Canada**

1. The Blessed Virgin Mary.
2. Christian Tradition.
3. St. Joachim.
4. He sent an angel.
5. The Shrine of St. Anne de Beaupré.

**St. Thomas the Apostle: Patron of India**

1. India.
2. He gave it to all the poor people of the kingdom.
3. He received a vision saying that Thomas had built a palace in Heaven for the king.
4. St. Thomas mainly preached to the poor.
5. They thought it was cursed (but, in reality, it was blessed).

**St. Denis: Patron of France**

1. Yes.
2. St. Dionysius.
3. Mercy.
4. Yes.
5. The kings of France were buried there for hundreds of years.

**St. Nicholas: Patron of Russia**

1. Saint Nicholas.
2. Heaven.
3. The first person to walk through the church door was to be the new bishop, and this man would be named Nicholas.
4. Miracles.
5. St. Nicholas appeared to him in a vision.

**St. Patrick: Patron of Ireland**

1. Pirates.
2. Ireland.
3. One hundred times a day and one hundred times a night.
4. A missionary to the Irish.
5. Monasteries and convents.

**St. Augustine of Canterbury: Patron of England**

1. Pope Gregory.
2. He turned them into Catholic churches.
3. Canterbury.
4. The Pope.
5. Yes.

**St. Willibrord: Patron of Holland**

1. England.
2. Yes.
3. He killed some of the plants and small animals for food.
4. No, some did not.
5. They hold hands and dance through the streets. They also receive a blessing at St. Willibrord's shrine.

**St. Boniface: Patron of Germany**

1. In an oak tree.
2. He chopped it down.
3. England.
4. Germany.
5. Many holy monks and nuns.

## St. Wenceslaus: Patron of Czechoslovakia

1. St. Wenceslaus' parents.
2. She was a saint—St. Ludmilla.
3. His mother.
4. His brother, Boleslaus.
5. To Mass.

## Saints Cyril and Methodius: Co-patrons of Europe

1. Yes, they were brothers.
2. Yes, for being very learned and holy men.
3. It had no alphabet.
4. Yes.
5. The Bible.

## St. Stephen: Patron of Hungary

1. Move from place to place.
2. Yes.
3. A beautiful crown.
4. Yes, even those who tried to murder him.
5. The Nazis.

## St. Francis of Assisi: Patron of Italy

1. Rich.
2. A soldier.
3. Yes.
4. Angry.
5. He could control the animals and cure the sick.

## St. Elizabeth:  Patroness of Portugal

1. Yes.
2. No.
3. When you do not choose whom you marry.
4. Peace.
5. She joined the convent of the Poor Clares. (She did not become a Poor Clare, but she lived with them according to their rule.)

## St. Bridget:  Patroness of Sweden

1. Christ.
2. She was married.
3. She was one of St. Bridget's children.
4. She became a nun.
5. She wrote a book, called *Revelations*, containing the private revelations given to her by Jesus and Mary.

## St. Francis Xavier:  Patron of the Orient

1. Souls.
2. The Jesuits.
3. India.
4. No, because any European who visited there risked death.
5. No, he died of a fever while waiting for permission to enter China.

## St. Rose of Lima:  Patroness of Latin America and the Philippines

1. Yes, she made a shed or hut in her backyard and spent many hours there alone in prayer.
2. She became very ill.
3. Yes, many men wanted to marry her.
4. Rose joined the convent of St. Dominic in Lima.
5. We learn the importance of a quiet life of prayer and penance.

## St. Peter Claver:  Patron of Colombia

1. He brought them blankets and medicine, cleaned them, cared for their wounds, and even held in his arms those with terrible diseases.
2. Yes, he felt God's call, but would rather have worked as a layman for Jesus.
3. Yes.
4. They had to tie him onto his horse so that he could go and see his people.
5. They broke into his room and took pieces of his clothing or bits of his possessions.

# Like our books?

You might like our program, too. Seton Home Study School offers a full curriculum program for Pre-Kindergarten through Twelfth Grade. We include daily lesson plans, answer keys, quarterly tests, and much more. Our staff of teachers and counselors is available to answer questions and offer help. We keep student records and send out diplomas that are backed by our accreditation with the Southern Association of Colleges and Schools and the AdvancEd Accreditation Commission.

For more information about Seton Home Study School,
please contact our admissions office.

**Seton Home Study School**
**1350 Progress Drive**
**Front Royal, VA 22630**

Phone: 540-636-9990 • Fax: 540-636-1602
Internet: www.setonhome.org • E-mail: info@setonhome.org